CELEBRATING THE NAME PATRICIA

Celebrating the Name Patricia

Walter the Educator

Silent King Books a WhichHead Imprint

Copyright © 2024 by Walter the Educator

All rights reserved. No part of this book may be reproduced in any manner whatsoever without written permission except in the case of brief quotations embodied in critical articles and reviews.

First Printing, 2024

Disclaimer
This book is a literary work; poems are not about specific persons, locations, situations, and/or circumstances unless mentioned in a historical context. This book is for entertainment and informational purposes only. The author and publisher offer this information without warranties expressed or implied. No matter the grounds, neither the author nor the publisher will be accountable for any losses, injuries, or other damages caused by the reader's use of this book. The use of this book acknowledges an understanding and acceptance of this disclaimer.

dedicated to everyone with the first name of Patricia

CONTENTS

Dedication v

One - Doth Shine 1

Two - Name Of Glory 3

Three - Dear Patricia 5

Four - Patricia's Name 7

Five - Filled With Wonder 9

Six - Hope And Love 11

Seven - Legacy To Sustain 13

Eight - Beyond Compare 15

Nine - Forever Thrive 17

Ten - Legacy So Pure 19

Eleven - Patricia, Like A Star 21

Twelve - Take The Lead 23

Thirteen - Blessing For All 25

Fourteen - Forever There 27

Fifteen - Name So Bright 29

Sixteen - Patricia's Sky 31

Seventeen - Presence Gleams 33

Eighteen - Dances On The Lips 35

Nineteen - Praise And Acclaim 37

Twenty - Patricia, Oh Patricia 39

Twenty-One - Name So Divine 41

Twenty-Two - Very Syllable 43

Twenty-Three - Cherished 45

Twenty-Four - Love And Light 47

Twenty-Five - Honor The Name Of
Patricia 49

Twenty-Six - Praises Of Patricia 51

Twenty-Seven - Rare And True 53

Twenty-Eight - Inspires Admiration 55

Twenty-Nine - Everlasting Embrace 57

Thirty - Power Of A Thousand Suns . . . 59

Thirty-One - Paragon Of Distinction . . . 61

Thirty-Two - Through The Ages 63

Thirty-Three - Undying Splendor 65

Thirty-Four - Elegance 67

Thirty-Five - Timeless Radiance 69

About The Author 71

ONE

DOTH SHINE

Patricia, oh how the name doth shine,
Like a precious gem in a golden mine,
A symphony of syllables, a melody divine,
In the garden of names, a rare and lovely vine.
With each letter, a story unfolds,
A tapestry of tales, untold and bold,
A name that dances, in the moonlit cold,
And whispers secrets, of the days of old.
Patricia, a beacon in the darkest night,
A flame of courage, burning bright,
A warrior's spirit, ready for the fight,
A constellation in the starry height.
In the chambers of the heart, it echoes true,
A name that carries the skies of blue,
A melody that sings, a morning dew,
A sweet embrace, for me and you.

Patricia, like a lighthouse on the shore,
Guiding ships to safety, forevermore,
A name that opens, a welcoming door,
A symphony of love, to adore.
So here's to Patricia, in all her grace,
A name that time cannot erase,
A treasure trove, in every space,
A masterpiece, in every place.

TWO

NAME OF GLORY

In the realm of names, there's none quite like Patricia,
A moniker of grace, a label so exquisite,
It dances on the tongue, a melody of syllables,
A name that echoes through the ages, timeless and formidable.

Patricia, oh Patricia, a name of regal bearing,
It sparkles in the sunlight, like diamonds in the morning,
A name that holds the secrets of ancient folklore,
A tapestry of history, a legacy to adore.

In gardens of language, Patricia blooms like a rose,
A symbol of elegance, a name that truly glows,
It resonates with power, a force to be reckoned,
A name that whispers strength, in every syllable beckoned.

Patricia, dear Patricia, a name so full of wonder,
It weaves through the fabric of time, never torn asunder,
A name that sings of wisdom, of knowledge and insight,
A beacon in the darkness, a guiding, radiant light.
So here's to Patricia, in all her splendor and grace,
A name that stands alone, in a wondrous, noble space,
A name that will endure, through every age and story,
For Patricia, dear Patricia, is truly a name of glory.

THREE

DEAR PATRICIA

Patricia, a name so rare, a symphony of syllables,
It dances on the wind, a melody so formidable,
A name that graces history, adorned with regal air,
A tapestry of elegance, beyond compare.

In the lexicon of names, Patricia stands tall,
A beacon of resilience, in every rise and fall,
It echoes through the ages, a timeless, cherished sound,
A name that weaves through hearts, with grace profound.

Patricia, oh Patricia, a name of strength and might,
A fortress of fortitude, in every daunting plight,
It whispers tales of triumph, of courage and resolve,
A name that shines like stardust, in which we all revolve.

In the garden of existence, Patricia blooms with

grace,
A flower of compassion, a presence to embrace,
It paints the world with kindness, a brush of gentle hues,
A name that sings of empathy, in every path we choose.

So here's to Patricia, in all her splendor and allure,
A name that lights the heavens, a legacy so pure,
A name that binds us all, in a tapestry of glory,
For Patricia, dear Patricia, is truly a wondrous story.

FOUR

PATRICIA'S NAME

Patricia, a name so fair and rare,
Like a delicate flower with petals to spare,
A melody that sings in the quiet air,
A name that's eternally beyond compare.

In the garden of names, Patricia blooms,
A symphony of letters, a tale that looms,
With grace and elegance, it gently resumes,
A name that sparkles, never consumes.

Patricia, a name that dances with light,
A constellation of stars in the velvet night,
A tapestry of dreams, woven just right,
A name that shines with all its might.

In every syllable, a story unfurls,
Of courage and kindness, of precious pearls,
In each letter, a universe swirls,
A name that in every heart, deeply hurls.

Patricia, a name like a river's flow,
A whisper of love, a radiant glow,
A name that in every language will grow,
A name that the world will forever know.

So let's raise a toast to Patricia's name,
Let it echo in the hall of fame,
For it deserves all the love and acclaim,
A name that will always remain the same.

FIVE

FILLED WITH WONDER

In a world of endless wonder, a name stands tall and true
It's Patricia, a name that shines like morning dew
With grace and strength, it stands alone, a beacon in the night
A name that's filled with power, a name that's pure delight

Patricia, oh Patricia, a melody so sweet
It dances on the wind and makes the heart complete
With every syllable spoken, the world becomes serene
For in the name of Patricia, there's a beauty yet unseen

A name that echoes through the ages, a name that's full of light
It weaves through time and space, and fills the world

with might
From ancient lands to modern times, its legacy remains
For in the name of Patricia, there's an everlasting flame

So let us raise our voices, and sing this name so grand
Let it soar through the heavens, and across the golden sand
For in the name of Patricia, there's a magic all its own
A name that's filled with wonder, a name that's brightly shown

So here's to you, dear Patricia, may your name forever shine
And may its beauty and its grace endure throughout all time

SIX

HOPE AND LOVE

Amidst the symphony of names, there's one that stands apart
It's Patricia, a name that sings with elegance and art
In every letter, a tale unfolds, of strength and grace combined
A name that's like a precious gem, a treasure of the mind
  Patricia, oh Patricia, a name that's full of light
It sparkles in the darkest night, a beacon burning bright
With each syllable, a universe is born within its sound
A name that's like a tapestry, with beauty tightly wound
  A name that's etched in history, with stories left untold
It echoes through the ages, a legacy to behold

In every corner of the world, its melody is heard
For in the name of Patricia, there's wisdom in each word
    So let us raise our voices, and honor this name so dear
Let it dance upon the wind, and banish every fear
For in the name of Patricia, there's a promise of new dawn
A name that's filled with hope and love, a name to lean upon
    So here's to you, dear Patricia, may your name forever reign
And may its essence touch the stars, and echo through the plain

SEVEN

LEGACY TO SUSTAIN

Patricia, a name that glows with radiant allure,
A melody that whispers through the fabric of time,
Each syllable a symphony, a tapestry of grace,
In the name of Patricia, a legacy sublime.

In gardens of letters, it blooms like a rare flower,
A name that dances on the tongue with sweet embrace,
With every utterance, a universe is unfurled,
In the name of Patricia, there's a boundless space.

A name imbued with stories, woven through history's loom,
It resonates in echoes, a timeless, resplendent tune,
From ancient realms to modern days, its echo reverberates,
In the name of Patricia, a saga that captivates.

Let us raise our voices, and sing of this name so

divine,
Let it soar across the heavens, and in the earthly chime,
For in the name of Patricia, there's a promise of new morn,
A name that's filled with wisdom, a name that's gently worn.

So here's to you, dear Patricia, may your name forever reign,
And may its essence permeate, a legacy to sustain,
For in the name of Patricia, there's a spirit that abides,
A name that's intertwined with beauty, where love and joy coincide.

EIGHT

BEYOND COMPARE

Patricia, a name that dances on the lips with grace,
A symphony of syllables that paints a timeless place,
In every letter, a story unfolds, of valor and delight,
In the name of Patricia, there's a spark that ignites.
Bearing the weight of history, it stands with regal poise,
A name that echoes through the ages, a melody that never cloys,
In each utterance, a universe is stirred, a legacy untold,
In the name of Patricia, a narrative of courage unfolds.
A name that weaves through time, with threads of strength and love,
It resonates in every heart, below and high above,
From ancient tales to modern days, its spirit carries

on,
In the name of Patricia, a legacy that's never gone.

So let us raise our voices, and honor this name so grand,
Let it ripple through the cosmos, across the sea and land,
For in the name of Patricia, there's a promise of new light,
A name that's filled with wisdom, a name that shines so bright.

Here's to you, dear Patricia, may your name forever reign,
And may its essence fill the world, a melody without a stain,
For in the name of Patricia, there's a beauty that's so rare,
A name that's wrapped in wonder, with a spirit beyond compare.

NINE

FOREVER THRIVE

Patricia, a name that echoes through the ages,
In every syllable, a tale of resilience and courage engages,
A name that resonates with strength and grace,
In the name of Patricia, a legacy we embrace.

In the tapestry of names, it shines like a radiant star,
A name that weaves through time, near and far,
With each intonation, a symphony of hope and might,
In the name of Patricia, a beacon of unwavering light.

From ancient realms to modern days, its melody endures,
A name that embodies wisdom, a spirit that assures,
Let us raise our voices, and sing of this name so grand,
For in the name of Patricia, there's a promise to understand.

Here's to you, dear Patricia, may your name forever thrive,
In the annals of history, may it eternally revive,
For in the name of Patricia, there's a beauty that transcends,
A name that's adorned with grace, a legacy that amends.

TEN

LEGACY SO PURE

Patricia, a name that sings of elegance and grace,
In the tapestry of names, it finds an exalted place,
With every syllable spoken, a tale of resilience is told,
In the name of Patricia, a story of strength and bold.

A name that echoes through time, with a melody so rare,
It dances through history, a legacy beyond compare,
From ancient lands to modern days, its echo reverberates,
In the name of Patricia, a saga that captivates.

Let us raise our voices, and celebrate this name so dear,
Let it soar through the cosmos, dispelling every fear,
For in the name of Patricia, there's a promise of new beginnings,

A name that's filled with hope and love, a melody worth spinning.

Here's to you, dear Patricia, may your name forever endure,
In the tapestry of existence, a legacy so pure,
For in the name of Patricia, there's a spirit that transcends,
A name that's adorned with beauty, where love and joy amends.

ELEVEN

PATRICIA, LIKE A STAR

Oh, Patricia, your name is a symphony,
A tapestry of letters, a masterpiece of harmony,
In the garden of names, you stand tall and bright,
A beacon of elegance, a radiant light.

With each letter, a story unfolds,
A cascade of beauty, a tale untold,
Patricia, oh, how your name enchants,
Like a melody that the heart implants.

Pristine and pure, like a mountain spring,
Your name dances on the tongue, a wondrous thing,
In the labyrinth of letters, you hold the key,
A name that's more than just a name, it's a melody.

In the canvas of names, you paint a picture so rare,
A name that whispers secrets in the midnight air,

Patricia, oh, how your name resounds,
A symphony of grace that knows no bounds.
  With each syllable, a dream takes flight,
A name that shines in the darkest night,
Patricia, like a star in the endless sky,
A name that's more than just a name, it's a lullaby.
  So, here's to you, Patricia, so dear,
A name that fills the heart with cheer,
In the grand tapestry of names, you reign,
A name that's more than just a name, it's a refrain.

TWELVE

TAKE THE LEAD

Oh, Patricia, a name so fine,
In the realm of names, it brightly shines,
Like a river flowing with grace and ease,
A name that dances in the gentle breeze.
In the tapestry of letters, it weaves a tale,
A name that's a symphony, never frail,
Patricia, oh, how your name resounds,
A melody of elegance that knows no bounds.
With each syllable, it paints a scene,
A name that's more than just a routine,
Patricia, like a star in the midnight sky,
A name that captures every passerby.
In the garden of names, it stands so tall,
A name that's a masterpiece, above all,
Patricia, oh, how your name ignites,
A spark of wonder, a cascade of lights.

Pristine and pure, like a mountain stream,
Your name is a vision, a heavenly dream,
In the chorus of names, it sings so clear,
A name that banishes every fear.

So, here's to you, Patricia, so grand,
A name that's a marvel, a name that's so grand,
In the symphony of names, you take the lead,
A name that's more than just a name, indeed!

THIRTEEN

BLESSING FOR ALL

Patricia, the name that dances on the lips,
A melody of syllables, a rhythm that skips.
In the garden of names, yours blooms with grace,
A symphony of letters, a portrait to embrace.
　A name that whispers of strength and might,
Of wisdom and beauty, a guiding light.
In the tapestry of names, yours shines like a gem,
A radiant star, a priceless diadem.
　Patricia, a name that weaves through time,
A legacy of courage, a verse that rhymes.
In the story of life, yours is a chapter bold,
A tale of resilience, a legend untold.
　With each letter, a story unfolds,
A journey of triumph, a destiny that molds.
Patricia, a name that paints the skies,
A canvas of dreams, a spirit that flies.

So here's to you, Patricia, with love and cheer,
A name that sparkles, a presence so dear.
In the tapestry of names, yours stands tall,
A beacon of hope, a blessing for all.

FOURTEEN

FOREVER THERE

Patricia, oh name so fair and rare,
In your beauty, none can compare.
Like a gentle breeze on a summer's day,
Your name brings joy in every way.

With syllables that dance and sing,
In every line, your name takes wing.
Patricia, a melody of grace,
In every heart, you find your place.

From ancient lands to modern shores,
Your name in history beautifully soars.
A symphony of letters, perfectly arranged,
In every language, your beauty is proclaimed.

Patricia, a name that shines so bright,
In every darkness, a guiding light.
In gardens of words, you bloom with pride,
A name that can never be denied.

In each letter, a story unfolds,
Of strength, kindness, and tales untold.
Patricia, a name with endless power,
In every moment, you truly tower.
   So let us raise our voices high,
And praise the name that touches the sky.
Patricia, a name beyond compare,
In every heart, forever there.

FIFTEEN

NAME SO BRIGHT

Patricia, a name so full of grace,
In every syllable, a wondrous embrace.
With each letter, a tale to be told,
A name that shimmers like precious gold.

In the symphony of names, you stand tall,
A timeless beauty, beloved by all.
In the garden of language, you bloom bright,
A name that fills the world with delight.

Patricia, a melody in the air,
A name that whispers, a name so rare.
In every verse, your presence is felt,
A name that makes every heart melt.

From the ancient past to the present day,
Your name has woven its elegant way.
In every culture, you hold a place,
A name that embodies beauty and grace.

In the tapestry of life, you're a vibrant thread,
A name that resonates, a name well said.
Patricia, in every language, you shine,
A name that stands the test of time.
So let us raise our voices high,
And sing the praises of Patricia, nigh.
For in this name, we find such delight,
A name that sparkles, a name so bright.

SIXTEEN

PATRICIA'S SKY

Of noble birth, a name so fair,
Patricia, a gem beyond compare.
A melody of elegance and grace,
In every heart, you find your place.

Patricia, a name that echoes true,
In every dream, in every view.
A symphony of strength and light,
Guiding us through the darkest night.

In every whisper of the wind,
In every touch, in every grin,
Patricia, your essence shines,
A rare and precious opaline.

Like a lily in a field of green,
Your presence is a wondrous scene.
A tapestry of wisdom, love, and care,
Patricia, a name beyond compare.

In every star that lights the sky,
In every tear, in every sigh,
Patricia, your spirit soars,
A beacon of hope forevermore.

So let us raise our voices high,
And sing the praise of Patricia's sky.
For in this world, so vast and wide,
Her name will forever be our guide.

SEVENTEEN

PRESENCE GLEAMS

In the garden of names, Patricia blooms,
A rare and precious flower that looms.
With petals of resilience and grace,
Her name adorns this earthly space.
   Patricia, a symphony of sound,
In every heartbeat, she is found.
A melody of strength and love,
A name that shines bright as stars above.
   In every tale of ancient lore,
In every quest for something more,
Patricia, your name resounds,
A treasure that forever astounds.
   Like a phoenix rising from the flame,
Patricia, you bear no shame.
Your spirit dances with the wind,
A name that eternally rescinds.

In every stroke of an artist's brush,
In every rhythmic, hopeful hush,
Patricia, your essence sings,
A name that carries noble wings.

So let us honor, let us praise,
The name of Patricia, in countless ways.
For in this world, so vast and grand,
Her name will forever stand.

In every whisper of the trees,
In every wave that meets the seas,
Patricia, your presence gleams,
A name beyond our wildest dreams.

EIGHTEEN

DANCES ON THE LIPS

Patricia, a name that dances on the lips
A symphony of syllables, a melody that skips
Through time and space, it echoes with grace
A name that holds a timeless place
In the garden of names, Patricia blooms
A flower of elegance, dispelling all glooms
With each letter, a story unfolds
Of strength, beauty, and tales untold
P - for the power that resides within
A - for the artistry that's akin
T - for the tenacity that never wanes
R - for the radiance that forever reigns
I - for the intelligence that shines so bright
C - for the compassion that brings delight
I - for the integrity that stands tall
A - for the allure that enthralls all

In the tapestry of names, Patricia weaves
A thread of resilience that never leaves
With every breath, a legacy is carved
Of courage, kindness, and love unbarred
So let the world sing the name of Patricia
A symphony of strength, a ballad of charisma
For in this name, a universe resides
Where grace and glory forever abides

NINETEEN

PRAISE AND ACCLAIM

In the garden of names, Patricia blooms,
A melody of syllables, a name that consumes.
With grace and elegance, it dances on the tongue,
A symphony of letters, a name that's never sung.
Patricia, oh Patricia, a name like no other,
A beacon of strength, a name to uncover.
In the tapestry of names, it shines like a star,
A name that's revered, no matter how far.
From the hills of old to the cities of new,
Patricia stands tall, in every shade and hue.
A name that evokes a sense of pride,
A name that resonates, far and wide.
In the chronicles of time, it stands the test,
A name that endures, among the best.

For in each syllable, a story is told,
Of courage and wisdom, of secrets unfold.
    Patricia, oh Patricia, a name of allure,
A name that's timeless, steadfast and pure.
So let us raise our voices, in praise and acclaim,
For Patricia, a name that will forever reign.

TWENTY

PATRICIA, OH PATRICIA

In the realm of names, Patricia gleams,
A cascade of letters, a name that dreams.
With a touch of mystique, it whispers in the wind,
A name that's cherished, where beginnings and ends begin.
Patricia, oh Patricia, a name so divine,
A tapestry of syllables, a name that intertwines.
In the sonnet of life, it resonates with grace,
A name that adorns, every time and space.
From ancient folklore to modern-day lore,
Patricia thrives, like never before.
A name that embodies resilience and might,
A name that ignites, a celestial light.
In the anthology of names, it stands tall and proud,
A name that echoes, amidst the crowd.

For within its essence, a legacy thrives,
Of valor and kindness, where every heart thrives.
    Patricia, oh Patricia, a name that reverberates,
A symphony of sounds, where love initiates.
So let us celebrate, in jubilant refrain,
For Patricia, a name that will forever sustain.

TWENTY-ONE

NAME SO DIVINE

In the realm of names, none shines as bright
As Patricia, a beacon of grace and might
A symphony of syllables, a melody so sweet
A name that makes the heart skip a beat

Patricia, a name that whispers in the wind
Carrying tales of strength and love, it's akin
To a rare and precious gem, a treasure untold
A name that stands out, a sight to behold

In the tapestry of names, Patricia weaves
A story of resilience, of dreams it achieves
A name that dances on the lips, a joy to say
It brings warmth and light, brightening the day

With each letter, a new chapter unfurls
A name that conquers, a name that twirls
In the garden of names, Patricia blooms
Radiant and unique, dispelling all glooms

 So here's to Patricia, a name so divine
A symphony of letters, a name that shines
In every verse, in every line, it stands tall
A name that echoes beauty, captivating all
 Embrace the magic, the wonder, the delight
For Patricia is a name that ignites
A fire within, a spark that never fades
A name that resonates, in sunlit glades

TWENTY-TWO

VERY SYLLABLE

In the garden of life, there blooms Patricia,
A name so rare, a gem so exquisite,
With a melody that dances on the wind,
A symphony of beauty, so wondrously intrinsic.
Patricia, a name that echoes through time,
A beacon of grace, a shimmering rhyme,
Like a star in the night, a guiding light,
She shines with elegance, a celestial sight.
In the tapestry of names, she's a masterpiece,
A stroke of brilliance, a wonder never to cease,
Her aura exudes warmth, like the sun's embrace,
A gentle breeze, a comforting solace.
In her eyes, the wisdom of ancient lore,
In her smile, the joy of a thousand more,
With every step, she paints the earth anew,
A muse of life, a canvas of hues so true.

Patricia, a name that whispers of strength,
A force of nature, a river's endless length,
She weaves resilience into every thread,
A tapestry of dreams, a tale to be read.
So here's to Patricia, a name so divine,
A treasure to cherish, a rare find,
In every syllable, a world to explore,
A name like no other, forever to adore.

TWENTY-THREE

CHERISHED

Patricia, a name so fair and fine,
In every syllable, a spark divine,
A melody that dances through the air,
A name that's beyond compare.

Patricia, with strength and grace,
A name that lights up every space,
Like a sunrise over the rolling sea,
A name that sets the spirit free.

In every letter, a story to be told,
Of courage, wisdom, and love so bold,
A name that echoes through the ages,
In history's grandest, noblest pages.

Patricia, a name of power and might,
A beacon in the darkest night,
A name that whispers of hope and light,
Guiding us through the endless flight.

In every sound, a promise so true,
Of loyalty and faith, like morning dew,
A name that shines like a precious gem,
A symbol of strength, a priceless diadem.

Patricia, a name that stands alone,
A masterpiece in every tone,
In every heartbeat, a rhythm so rare,
A name beyond compare.

So let us raise our voices high,
And sing the praises of Patricia's sky,
For in this name, we find our song,
A name that's cherished all along.

TWENTY-FOUR

LOVE AND LIGHT

In the realm of names, there's one that reigns,
A symphony of letters, a melody that sustains,
Patricia, a name so regal and rare,
A tapestry of beauty beyond compare.
   In each syllable, a tale unfolds,
Of strength and kindness, as history beholds,
A name that echoes through time's embrace,
A beacon of grace, a celestial trace.
   Patricia, a name that blooms and thrives,
In every heart, its essence connives,
A name that resonates with love and light,
A constellation of virtues shining bright.
   In every consonant, a whisper of might,
A name that conquers the darkest night,
A gentle breeze, a fierce wildfire,
A name that fills every heart's desire.

Patricia, a name that paints the sky,
With hues of courage and dreams that fly,
A name that dances in the cosmic ballet,
A lighthouse in the tempest's sway.

In each phoneme, a universe unfurls,
Of wisdom, compassion, and unfaltering pearls,
A name that weaves a tapestry so grand,
A masterpiece crafted by fate's own hand.

So let us raise our voices high,
And let the name of Patricia touch the sky,
For in this name, we find a treasure rare,
A name beyond compare.

TWENTY-FIVE

HONOR THE NAME OF PATRICIA

Patricia, a name of elegance and grace,
In every syllable, a gentle embrace,
A melody that dances on the breeze,
A symphony of beauty that forever frees.
   In each letter, a story to be told,
Of resilience, kindness, and wisdom bold,
A name that echoes through the ages past,
A legacy of strength that eternally lasts.
   Patricia, a name that blooms like a rare flower,
In every season, it holds steadfast power,
A name that resonates with love and light,
A constellation of virtues shining bright.
   In every sound, a promise of hope,
A beacon of strength to help us cope,

With every challenge that comes our way,
Patricia's name is there to light the day.

Patricia, a name that paints the sky,
With hues of courage that soar up high,
A name that whispers of dreams untold,
A compass of love in a world so bold.

In each phoneme, a symphony of grace,
A name that time and again, love will embrace,
A name that weaves a tapestry so fine,
A masterpiece of destiny, a name divine.

So let us raise our voices in jubilation,
And honor the name of Patricia, a celebration,

TWENTY-SIX

PRAISES OF PATRICIA

    Amidst the fields of emerald green
Stands a lady fair, with eyes serene
Patricia, her name doth ring
Like a sweet melody, a song to sing
    In her presence, all worries fade
As if touched by a gentle cascade
Her laughter, like a bubbling brook
Brings joy to hearts with every look
    Patricia, a name so rare and true
Like a rare gem, with a radiant hue
A beacon of hope in the darkest night
Guiding lost souls towards the light
    With wisdom deep as the ocean's floor
She weaves tales of love and lore
Her words, like a soothing balm
Healing wounds with their gentle calm

In her gaze, the stars find their glow
And the moon, its ethereal flow
Patricia, a name that holds such grace
A blessing to behold, in every place
So let us raise our voices high
And sing the praises of Patricia, nigh
For in her name, we find delight
A symphony of joy, so pure and bright

TWENTY-SEVEN

RARE AND TRUE

Amidst the bustling city streets, there walks a woman fair
With grace and elegance, she moves as if through the open air
Patricia, her name shines bright, like the morning sun
A beacon of hope, a guiding light for everyone
In her eyes, the wisdom of ages past
A gentle spirit, a love that will forever last
Patricia, a name so rare and true
A melody of kindness, a symphony of virtue
With every step, she leaves a trail of kindness in her wake
Like a field of flowers, blooming for love's sake
Her laughter, a melody that dances on the wind
Bringing joy and solace to those who have sinned
Patricia, a name that carries strength and grace

A shield against the darkness, a warm and loving embrace
In her presence, troubles melt away
As if touched by the dawn of a brand new day
    So let us raise a toast to Patricia, fair and kind
A soul so pure, a heart so finely twined
For in her name, we find a love so true
A radiant light, shining bright for me and you

TWENTY-EIGHT

INSPIRES ADMIRATION

In the realm of dreams, there dwells a maiden fair
With a name that echoes through the misty air
Patricia, her name a tapestry of grace
A melody of strength, a vision of beauty to embrace
In her gaze, the stars find their reflection
A symphony of love, a boundless affection
Patricia, a name that carries a timeless charm
A lighthouse of hope, amidst the raging storm
Her laughter, like a chorus of morning birds
Bringing warmth and joy with every word
Patricia, a name so rare and true
A sanctuary of kindness, a haven for the weary few
With every step, she paints the world with light
A masterpiece of love, shining ever bright

Her presence, a soothing balm for troubled souls
A healing touch, mending shattered goals
    Patricia, a name that holds a secret power
A gentle strength that blooms like a midnight flower
So let us raise our voices in celebration
Of Patricia, a name that inspires admiration
    For in her name, we find a universe of love
A symphony of grace, descending from above
Patricia, a name that weaves a timeless tale
Of kindness, resilience, and love that will never fail

TWENTY-NINE

EVERLASTING EMBRACE

Amidst the rolling hills and meadows wide
Stands a woman with a spirit deep and wide
Patricia, her name a melody divine
A symphony of strength, a beacon that will shine
In her eyes, the wisdom of ancient lore
A gentle soul, a heart that does implore
Patricia, a name so rare and true
A canvas of compassion, a vista of virtue
With every smile, she paints the world aglow
A masterpiece of love, a river's gentle flow
Her laughter, a chorus of joyous delight
Bringing solace and warmth, like a starry night
Patricia, a name that carries grace and might
A sanctuary of hope, a haven in the night

In her presence, troubles find their peaceful rest
As if cradled by the moon in its silver crest
   So let us raise our voices in sweet acclaim
For Patricia, a name that ignites love's flame
In her name, we find a universe of light
A tapestry of kindness, a beacon burning bright
   Patricia, a name that weaves a tale so fine
Of resilience, compassion, and love that will shine
In her name, we find a symphony of grace
A portrait of strength, an everlasting embrace

THIRTY

POWER OF A THOUSAND SUNS

In the garden of the mind, Patricia blooms,
A name that dances on the tongue like a melody,
A symphony of syllables, a tapestry of letters,
A name that whispers secrets to the wind.
Patricia, the keeper of wisdom and grace,
Her name a star in the night sky of possibility,
A beacon of hope in the stormy seas of life,
A lighthouse guiding souls to safety.
In the tapestry of time, Patricia's name is woven,
Threads of courage, threads of compassion,
A name that echoes through the corridors of history,
A name that weaves its way into the fabric of our hearts.
Patricia, a name that sparkles like a diamond,
A name that shimmers like the morning dew,

A name that sings like a choir of angels,
A name that dances like a flame in the darkness.
In the language of love, Patricia's name is spoken,
A symphony of affection, a sonnet of adoration,
A name that blooms in the garden of the heart,
A name that will forever be cherished and adored.
So let us raise our voices and celebrate,
The name of Patricia, a name like no other,
A name that holds the power of a thousand suns,
A name that will never fade, but only grow brighter.

THIRTY-ONE

PARAGON OF DISTINCTION

In the realm of names, Patricia reigns supreme,
A regal melody that graces all who utter it,
A name adorned with the opulence of elegance,
A tapestry of letters woven with utmost care.
Patricia, a name that resonates with resilience,
A moniker that carries the weight of valor and virtue,
An emblem of fortitude in the face of adversity,
A beacon of strength amid life's tempestuous seas.
In the annals of time, Patricia's name stands tall,
A testament to the enduring spirit of humanity,
A name that echoes through the corridors of legacy,
A name that etches itself into the tapestry of existence.
Patricia, a name that glimmers like precious jewels,
A name that exudes the allure of timeless grace,

A name that dances in the hearts of those who speak it,
A symphony of syllables that enraptures the senses.

In the language of reverence, Patricia's name is heralded,
A sonnet of admiration, an ode to unwavering poise,
A name that blossoms in the gardens of admiration,
A name that kindles the fires of fervent admiration.

So let us raise our voices in jubilation,
For the name of Patricia, a paragon of distinction,
A name that embodies the essence of magnificence,
A name that shall endure through the annals of time.

THIRTY-TWO

THROUGH THE AGES

Patricia, a name that sings with gentle grace,
A melody that whispers through the winds of time,
A symphony of syllables that dance in harmony,
A name that adorns the lips with elegance.

In the tapestry of existence, Patricia's name shines,
A beacon of compassion in the labyrinth of life,
An emblem of resilience in the face of trials,
A lighthouse guiding souls to tranquil shores.

Patricia, a name that blooms like a rare orchid,
A fragrance that lingers in the corridors of memory,
A name that paints the canvas of dreams with hope,
A constellation of letters that maps out destiny.

In the language of love, Patricia's name resonates,
A sonnet of admiration, a ballad of tenderness,
A name that blossoms in the garden of affection,
A name that ignites the flames of ardent devotion.

So let us raise our voices in celebration,
For the name of Patricia, a jewel in the crown of existence,
A name that embodies the virtues of nobility,
A name that shall endure through the ages with unwavering grace.

THIRTY-THREE

UNDYING SPLENDOR

Patricia, a name that unfolds like a rare blossom,
A symphony of syllables that captivate the soul,
A tapestry of letters intricately woven with care,
A name that exudes an aura of timeless elegance.

In the mosaic of life, Patricia's name glows,
A guiding star in the constellation of humanity,
An emblem of courage amidst tumultuous tides,
A sanctuary of warmth in the coldest of nights.

Patricia, a name that shimmers like a moonlit lake,
A melody that lingers in the chambers of memory,
A name that paints the sky with hues of resilience,
A lighthouse guiding wanderers to safe havens.

In the language of reverence, Patricia's name resounds,
A sonnet of admiration, an anthem of strength,

A name that blossoms in the garden of inspiration,
A name that kindles the fire of unwavering spirit.
   So let us raise our voices in jubilation,
For the name of Patricia, a treasure of distinction,
A name that embodies the essence of enduring grace,
A name that shall echo through eternity with undying splendor.

THIRTY-FOUR

ELEGANCE

Patricia, a name that glistens like a dew-kissed petal,
A sonnet of syllables that dances on the breeze,
A mosaic of letters that form a masterpiece,
A name that resonates with a timeless allure.
In the tapestry of existence, Patricia's name reigns,
A sanctuary of compassion in a world of chaos,
An embodiment of resilience in the face of adversity,
A guiding light through the labyrinth of life.
Patricia, a name that sparkles like a starlit sky,
A melody that lingers in the chambers of the heart,
A name that paints the universe with hues of hope,
A beacon of solace in the darkest of nights.
In the language of adoration, Patricia's name thrives,
A ballad of admiration, a serenade of fortitude,
A name that blooms in the garden of inspiration,

A name that ignites the flames of unwavering devotion.
So let us raise our voices in exaltation,
For the name of Patricia, a paragon of distinction,
A name that embodies the virtues of graciousness,
A name that shall endure through the ages with unwavering elegance.

THIRTY-FIVE

TIMELESS RADIANCE

In the tapestry of time, Patricia's name is woven,
A symphony of elegance in the grand opera of existence,
An emblem of fortitude amidst the tempest of life,
A radiant beacon guiding souls to tranquil shores.

Patricia, a name that glistens like a diamond in the sun,
An echo that resonates in the halls of remembrance,
A name that paints the sky with hues of resilience,
A sanctuary of warmth in the coldest of nights.

In the language of admiration, Patricia's name sings,
A sonnet of reverence, a paean to unwavering spirit,
A name that blossoms in the garden of adoration,
A flame that kindles the fire of fervent devotion.

So let us raise our voices in celebration,
For the name of Patricia, a testament to grace,

A name that embodies the essence of enduring elegance,
A name that shall endure through the ages with timeless radiance.

ABOUT THE AUTHOR

Walter the Educator is one of the pseudonyms for Walter Anderson. Formally educated in Chemistry, Business, and Education, he is an educator, an author, a diverse entrepreneur, and he is the son of a disabled war veteran. "Walter the Educator" shares his time between educating and creating. He holds interests and owns several creative projects that entertain, enlighten, enhance, and educate, hoping to inspire and motivate you.

Follow, find new works, and stay up to date
with Walter the Educator™
at WaltertheEducator.com

www.ingramcontent.com/pod-product-compliance
Lightning Source LLC
LaVergne TN
LVHW052000060526
838201LV00059B/3757